LOVE AND LIES: THE 9 MYTHS OF INDIAN MARRIAGES

A GUIDE TO REFLECT YOUR MARRIAGE, SOME MYTHS OF MARRIAGE ARE EXPOSED OF

SAMATHA REDDY

Clever Fox®
PUBLISHING
Chennai • Bangalore

CLEVER FOX PUBLISHING
Chennai, India

Published by CLEVER FOX PUBLISHING 2025

ISBN: 978-93-7500-410-3

INTRODUCTION

As a young girl, I attended many weddings — of my uncles, aunts, and cousins.
From the audience seats, marriage always looked like a fairy tale.

Grand celebrations.
Blessings showered generously.
The bride and groom admired each other with shy smiles and stolen glances.
There was tenderness — a hidden charm that felt sacred and beautiful.

But when I met the same couples a few years later, something felt different.

The charm had faded.
The chemistry felt replaced by heaviness.
What I saw instead were tired faces, unspoken resentment, and endless complaints.

When I asked what had changed, the answers were familiar: responsibilities, EMIs, family pressure, unmet expectations, disappointment with each other — often expressed as blame.

This became a quiet mystery for me.

I believed my marriage would be different.
I told myself I would make it as beautiful as a fairy tale.

This belief took root in me as a young adult, just after my teenage years.

And then… life happened.

Despite my continuous efforts, I too experienced the fading charm in my own marriage.
My relationship became a rainbow of laughter, pain, blame, romance, responsibility, love, and resentment — looping endlessly.

In conversations with friends, colleagues, siblings, and later my clients, I realized something unsettling:
we were all running the same emotional loop.

This led me into deep self-inquiry.

I carried one persistent question within me:
What truly changes in a couple's life — before and after marriage?

Over time, I began to understand that most of us (including myself) enter marriage carrying certain myths and expectations.
As years pass, reality confronts these beliefs — and when we resist accepting it, we slowly lose the essence of marriage itself:
companionship and teamwork.

This book is my attempt to expose the basic myths with which many Indian marriages begin.
Some chapters may feel uncomfortable.
Some may pause you into reflection.
This book is meant to act as a mirror — not to judge your relationship, but to help you see it clearly.

Marriage is the sweetest adventure that can also feel like the toughest exam you were never prepared for.
One day you feel like a celebrity in love.
The next, you silently wonder, "Why did I even marry?"

From the weddings we admired as children to the marriages we now navigate, many of us have whispered at some point:
"Maybe everyone else's marriage is happier than mine."

Drawing from years of observing families, friendships, and coaching relationships, this book uncovers the 9 Myths of Indian Marriage — invisible beliefs that quietly shape how we love, fight, adjust, and forgive.

With honesty, warmth, and gentle humor, this book invites you to question the "shoulds" that govern your marriage and rediscover love beyond rituals, roles, and expectations.

Whether you are single, newly married, or decades into marriage — this is not just a book to read.
It is a mirror to hold up to your relationship.

Because marriages are not made in heaven.
They are made right here — one honest conversation at a time.

CONTENTS

CHAPTER 1

THE PURPOSE - KAIKU SHADI KIYARE?

Pooja loved weddings as a child. She never missed a chance to attend.

Her two reasons to attend weddings are:

1. She loved the food (especially meals on a banana leaf).
2. She loved sitting right behind the aunties and listening to their gossip.

For news, who needs TV when you have aunties?

But in all that chatter, there was one line she heard over and over again:

"Vadina, ma abbayiki bhojanam ibbandi avuthundi, Pune lo vadu okkade vuntadu, he needs someone to cook. Dhobi is so costly anta, anduke we are planning to marry him off."

[English version: "Sister, my son works in Pune and he has two major challenges. The first challenge is with food. He eats every day from the hotel and has no one to cook at home. Second

Challenge is with laundry; those services are costly in Pune it seems. As a solution for these two challenges, we are looking for a bride to marry him off".]

Or sometimes:

"Bhabhi, Kishore ka aadat bura hai—raat ko friends ke saath idhar udhar… usko ghar ka khana chahiye. Kitna girlfriends ka chakkar chalega? Ek na ek din tho shaadi karna hai. Isliye maine ye ladki chunli. Gori hai, bahut kaam karti hai, kuch bhi nahi bolti—goongi nahi hai, kuch bhi sahan krleti hai."

[English version: "Sister, my son Kishore got into bad company, bad habits. He has many girlfriends, it's time for him to stop these affairs and get married. Adding to this, he eats hotel food. It's time for him to marry. I chose this girl (shows photo on mobile), she is the right one for Kishore. The girl is very fair, less talkative.

She can handle all household chores and has lots of patience to handle challenges".]

And then the classic line from a young man:

"Are mama, life bore kodtundi ra. Online lo ammayilni choosthe em labham? Nakosam oka ammayi vundali. Nenu nidra leche sariki naku coffee chese ammayi— evening intiki ochesariki saree kattukuni nakosam wait chesedi—naku kaavali."

[English version: "Hey brother, life is so boring now. There is no point in dating online. I want a girl in real life. The moment I wake up from bed, she must offer coffee to me, and how beautiful if she waits for my return from office in a saree. How lucky am I going to be?".]

Every time she heard it, Pooja thought to herself:

"OMG, I will never get married in arranged marriages."

"If this is marriage, better I stick to my banana leaf meals forever."

REFLECT:

"How many of us have seen marriages treated like a quick fix rather than a partnership?"

Because to them, marriage was like Dolo 650—one pill for everything.
Fever? Dolo. Cold? Dolo. Headache? Dolo. Can't sleep? Dolo.

These are some classic reasons for marriages I heard from people.

My Son is lonely and bored. - Get him married.
My Son Doesn't get to eat home-cooked meals? - Get him married.
My Son is a spoilt brat, and only his wife can correct him. - Get him married.
My family inheritance must continue - so my son must marry.
My Son has girlfriend from a different country, or out of caste, or out of state, or not in the same religion --Get him married to our Indian girl or a girl from our caste or religion, at least a girl who speaks our language.

My daughter is touching 30 years, it's too late - Get her married.
My daughter is traveling out of the country - it's better to marry her off before she leaves.
My daughter is too pretty, and I'm afraid her colleagues would propose to her - it's better she marries as soon as possible.
My daughter is becoming too fat day by day - better marry her off, it's difficult to find her groom.
My daughter is not so good-looking, she must marry at a young age, later she will never get the right groom.
Daughter is too independent— Get her married - Men don't like independent girls.

Marriage = solution for all problems.

But to Pooja, that sounded wrong. How could you drag another person's entire life into your emptiness? How could "marriage" be the medicine for boredom, bad habits, or loneliness?

Funny enough, she was thankful to those aunties and uncles.

Their gossip had opened her eyes. She made herself a promise:

"If I marry, it will be for love, for companionship, not for someone's laundry or coffee."

Soon, she met Venu at work. He was kind, funny, and genuinely enjoyed her company. Venu and Pooja worked on same project for 8 months. Venu helped Pooja many times in fixing bugs in her code.

They did pair-programming for many modules; in fact, her team started referring to them as *"THE PAIR"*.

This soon became reality, Venu and Pooja dated, laughed, and shared meals for the next two years.

Pooja felt safe, assured—*finally, this was love, not a deal.* With blessings from their families, they married.

When Dreams Meet Reality:

Pooja expected apples from life, but she got oranges.

For her, Marriage means: endless romance, Friday night movies, long weekend drives, cooking together just like they show in Movies.

"She thought marriage was an extension of dating life,

but reality came with extra characters—*the in-laws.*"

She didn't know, living with her in-laws means: Adjusting to new rules, and endless "training" from her mother-in-law.

The Mother-in-law's unasked training includes,

How to cook Venu's favourite dishes, how to dress to impress him.

How to receive relatives, how not to talk to her own parents every day.

she trained Pooja, how to forget her own parents, as after marriage, in-laws are her newborn parents.

One evening, after a long day at work, Pooja and Venu returned home exhausted.

Venu's mother handed him a glass of fresh juice, but none for her.

He relaxed in front of the TV "as if he had cut a huge mountain with his own hands,"

Pooja, watching the juice glass sweating in Venu's hand, her own throat becomes dry, and the clatter of utensils calls her back to the kitchen to join her mother-in-law in the kitchen. She missed her own mother's care.

The dream of partnership—cooking together, sharing chores, waiting for each other—felt like it was vanishing.

That night, staring at the ceiling, Pooja's heart sank.

"Whether it's love marriage or arranged marriage, why do people marry for the wrong reasons?

"I wanted a companion, not a cage. Her mind asked her Kaiku shaadi kiyare…"

"As a child, Pooja thought marriage was gossip entertainment."

"But as an adult, she discovered—it can become gossip itself, if you enter it for the wrong reasons."

Myth vs Fact

Myth:

Marriagc is likc *Dolo 650*— onc-stop solution for all your problems. Feeling lonely? Get married. Can't cook? Get married. Want entertainment? Get married.

Fact:

Marriage is not a medicine, not a shortcut, and not a cure. It doesn't erase bad habits or guarantee happiness. Real love

and lasting partnership demand daily effort—listening, respecting, growing together. Without that, even the strongest love can fade, and what remains is just duty, routine, or worse, betrayal. So, find your true reason to marry.

It means before you say yes, ask yourself:

REFLECT:

"Kaiku shadi kiyare - What is your purpose of marriage? –(if already married).
"Are you marrying to share life—or to solve a problem?" – (if you are planning to marry).

CHAPTER 2

YOU ARE MY WORLD - THE ILLUSION

"What happens when love flows like a flood from one side, but the other side is a silent desert?"

This is the story of Meena and Sundar - ***one-sided love in marriage.***

College Days

Meena and Sundar were classmates in engineering.

Sundar was the college topper—handsome, serious, never fighting with anyone.
Meena was the opposite—talkative, bubbly, the life of the class. She planned the outings, dragged everyone to movies, bunked lectures, and laughed the loudest.

From the first year, Meena had noticed Sundar, and she has deep admiration for him.

She kept her feelings a secret, but inside, she was overconfident: *"No one can dislike me. I deserve the BEST. And that's Sundar."*

Sundar, meanwhile, liked a few girls in class—Meena was one among them —but never dared to say anything. He kept everything locked inside.

Finally, in the last year, Meena couldn't hold it any longer.

She marched up to him and said,

"I love you, Sundu. I'm madly in love with you, and I can only think of marrying you."

Sundar smiled at her confession; he admires her boldness, yet feels unprepared.

Sundar only said, “Let’s see Meena, how it goes.”

Meena assumed this was Sundar’s way of accepting her Love. She is excited.

From then on, her days revolved around him.

Every morning, as soon as she opened her eyes, she would send messages:

“Good morning, Sundu baby.”

“I love you.”

“What color shirt are you wearing? Let’s twin today.”

“What is your breakfast?”

“I’m waiting to see you.”

“I’m waiting for our first touch.”

“Please don’t say no to me.”

“I can’t live without you.”

Meena never waited for his reply.

REFLECT

“Do you text to express—or to control?”

She just had to express her emotions—it was like a rule written in her heart. Since childhood, she’d been told,

"Meena, you must always say what you feel, don't hide anything." And she has followed it since then.

REFLECT

"How many of you are like Meena here?

"You just don't give space for others to think, because deep down you can't accept rejection."

Sundar, however, was overwhelmed. He rarely used to open WhatsApp—he used to open only when he was ten minutes away from college. His mind was on assignments, lab exams, and the pressure of getting placed.

He often thought,

"Do I even like anyone enough to marry?' Maybe it's too early. First, I need to settle, earn, buy a flat, support my sisters… marriage is too early to commit."

But he never said it. He didn't have the guts to reject Meena.

Deep inside, he feared—*what if no other girl ever liked me?*

REFLECT

"How many of you suffer saying No"?

"How many of our elders innocently trained us to become people pleasers?

"Do you accept every request - only then you're called good".

Married Life

They got placed through campus interviews. Sundar landed a top product company, earning double of what Meena made. But she was happier for his success than her own.

For her, life was simple: ***her world was Sundar.***

Her dreams repeated like a playlist on loop:

Meena is hugging and kissing Sundar.

Meena is cooking for Sundar.

Meena is washing and folding his clothes.

Meena is booking a new bike for him with half her salary.

She would smile at her phone every morning, typing: *"Good morning, Sundu baby."*

REFLECT

"Have you ever felt drowned in someone's love?"

Meena lived for him.

Meena breathed for him.

Meena became completely ***Sundar-oriented and zero self-oriented.***

Meena managed everything—office, cooking, chores, caring for their baby. She would wake up at midnight, feed the child, give the right dose of *crocin medicine*, and never once disturb Sundar's sleep because ***"he works so hard."***

She hoped ***"one day Sundar would feel himself lucky and would say, he got the world's most loving wife".***

Her hope remained as hope in reality.

She justified her disappointment - ***"Sundar actually loves me but doesn't know how to express".***

She self-declared, ***"Nobody can love Sundar like I do, not even his mother".***

But Sundar felt different. He didn't know how to say it, but her constant messages, her hovering—even knocking on the bathroom door asking, ***"Are you fine, Sundu?"***—felt suffocating.

He had never been hungry for love;

Now he felt drowned in it. He craved space, silence, air.

One day, he snapped.

"Meena, stop this overacting of love! You never gave me a chance to express myself."

"You assume everything you do is love, but I feel suffocated. I need some space."

He booked a solo trip to Manali, desperate for peace.

Meena was silent and frozen: Her phone was still glowing with her unread messages sent to him.

She whispered to herself, heartbroken and eyes wet:

"But I only loved him…No one loves Sundar more than I do."

Myth vs Fact

Myth:

"You are my world." To love someone is to live only for them, to give them your every breath, every dream, every ounce of yourself.

Fact:

When one person becomes your ***entire world***, you slowly ***lose your own self.***

Love thrives not in obsession but in balance.

A healthy marriage means two complete individuals choosing to share life.

Not one person disappearing into the other.

CHAPTER 3

MARRIAGES MADE IN HEAVEN

Weddings often look like heaven on earth. Grand venues glitter with lights and flowers, music fills the air, and photographers chase every moment. The tasty and unlimited buffet invites us to enjoy the feast.

Parents beam with satisfaction; they have ticked their life's big agenda - "Getting their children married off". While Cousins and relatives parade in silk sarees, diamonds, and heavy jewellery, competing in the unspoken contest of "who wore it best." The unmarried cousins request the photographers for best shots - the focus is, they must look beautiful, slim, and fair in the photographs.

Yes, this scene is festive and beautiful. It makes the newlyweds believe again that
"Marriages are made in Heaven".

For the bride and groom, it feels magical. Honeymoon days extend the illusion. They are deeply focused on each other. Their happy hormones are fully functional, and there are secret prayers to extend the honeymoon. They are far from home -far from reality.

The fresh breeze, the car parked facing mountains, and holding each other's hands make them experience "Yes, marriages are made in heaven".

But just as honeymoons fade, so does the "heaven phase." Newlyweds come home, and their love is still fiery, hormones are loyal, and every now and then, secret dates are continued. EMIs knock on the door, bosses flood inboxes with customer escalations, nearing release dates, and mothers from both sides want their share of attention.

As months turn into anniversaries, the thrill of discovery slowly dries up. One morning, they look at each other and realize there's nothing new left to explore. That's when an uninvited guest walks in— "boredom." It arrives quietly, settles like dust, and refuses to leave. The first set of hormones has taken its vacation, and now the second shift reports to duty—the ones that trigger irritation, over-analysis, and disappointment. The couple wonders:

Is this marriage, or a never-ending shift rotation of hormones?

At work, the storm is already brewing—customer escalations, grey-haired managers nagging about buggy products, and a few "creative" ones inventing new excuses to delay releases. By the time he clocks out, his head is heavy with office politics. But little does he know, another storm is waiting at home—and this one is called "family politics."

The moment he steps inside, a tsunami of complaints pours over him:

"Your mom does not like my cooking!"
"Your wife doesn't know anything!"
"She wakes up late!"
"Only I have to do everything!"
@$@#%$#^$%...

The poor "Groom Husband" looks helplessly at his father, sitting quietly in a corner with a newspaper. Without saying a word, the father signals: 'Be patient. This storm too shall pass.' Years of practice have made him fluent in this silent language, one his son has yet to learn.

He knows too well the power his mother wields. One wrong word, and her arsenal of silent treatments and emotional blackmail will rain down. So, with folded hands and a nervous smile, he turns to his wife:

"Honey, please adjust… just follow whatever she says. Practice perfecting those round rotis… and maybe let her keep the TV remote too."

The mother beams, proud that the power in this house still runs through her—not from BESCOM, but from her son's obedience.

Now comes the wife's turn. She, too, is trained in the art of silent treatment, in the natural flow of tears that arrive every time she recalls his judgment. The man she once called sweetheart now looks like "Mumma's Robot." Lonely in her own home, she clutches her phone, pouring her agony into long calls with her mother and whispered chats with her friends. Each tear, each complaint, is proof that the heaven they once dreamt of is slipping further away.

REFLECT

"When did love become a three-player game—husband, wife, and mother-in-law?"

This slowly diminishes the quality time they once craved. The movie nights vanish, and the long drives become rare memories. What remains are bare-minimum engagements in the bedroom, sudden hunger strikes, and endless binge-watching of web series with faces lit only by screens, not smiles. Everything starts looking dull, tasteless, repetitive—and in between, uncontrollable tears spill without warning. The same eyes that once sparkled with desire now search for silence.

REFLECT

"How many couples replace conversations with screens, and call it togetherness?"

One night, lying back-to-back, they turn away from each other. The question hangs heavy in both minds:
"Are marriages really made in Heaven?" Their hearts whisper rebellion: "No… It's a big lie. This feels more like hell."

"*If this is heaven, why does it suffocate so much?*

The mind smirks cruelly:

"Welcome to the world of Reality. This is why I kept warning you—don't overdose on movies. Reel life ends in credits, but real life begins after them."

This hide-and-seek of hormones keeps tossing them between Heaven and Hell. One day they laugh, the next day they burn in silence. It leaves them confused, anxious, staring into an uncertain future: "*What may happen in the coming years?"* Instead of reaching for each other, they reach for opinions. Judgments harden into cement, walls build slowly, and life is dragged along like luggage they no longer wish to carry but can't let go of.

REFLECT

"*Do we ever realize how opinions harden faster than love softens?"*

Myth: Marriages are made in Heaven.

Fact: Marriages are built on the ground. Two people can create Heaven or Hell in the same house—sometimes on the same day. The choice lies in whether they drop their opinions, speak their truth, and listen without judgment. Only then can marriage be navigated, not endured.

It's time to reflect on what your truth is...

CHAPTER 4

MY MONEY IS YOUR MONEY IN MARRIAGE

What's your equation about money in marriage?

How unique are we as humans? No human is alike, and each is unique.
Similarly, every couple creates a unique money equation, and it evolves as they grow older in relationships.

"In some marriages, love can sometimes be experienced like a transaction — the more one brings to the table, the more attention seems to flow. Not all attention is love, yet in its glow we often forget the difference."

They say "Love is Blind", but is love really blind to money?

Let's look at Sudha and Vijay's story.

Sudha and Vijay are both working. Vijay earns a few thousand more than her. When newly married, their focus was not money – it's about intimacy, impressing each other. who books movie tickets, who plans an anniversary vacation, and who pays bills at the hotel were not accounted for. It was a pleasure spending for each other. They were deeply in love with each other.

It's been 10 years since she was working. She made a job as her Identity. Her parents & in-laws were proud that their daughter is a working woman. There was respect, name among relatives.

Sudha is an emotional being, while Vijay is practical. They both are from different backgrounds - Vijay being the elder son, he has seen the financial challenges his joint family faced and closely watched his father managing. His father taught Vijay how to manage money. On the other hand, Sudha is the younger daughter; she had never gotten No for any of her requests. Her parents had not shared any knowledge about finances. She was the pampered daughter of a middle-class family.

Sudha, while she was in a job, was carefree about expenses, savings, and it was Vijay who made some savings and some vision. They had never sat together, planned, or discussed money. They allowed life to be a free flow.

After a few years recession hit the market - Sudha's company fired 400 employees, and she is one among them. Now Sudha is suddenly jobless, she became clueless about what to do whole day when there is no job. She felt empty inside. There was boredom, shame, and an identity crisis in her.

Reality had hit their lives. Now everything is accounted for - the frequency of watching movies together has dropped. Vijay suddenly becomes health-conscious, and he prefers home food more now. But Sudha is craving to eat her favourite biryani, Pani puri, and she wants to visit the Kerala mess.

REFLECT

"Have you noticed how finances quietly dictate the companionship in your own relationship?

Vijay started calculating how to save Maids salary- he looks at Sudha and says -
"See, you are not keeping yourself active.",
"You must do some physical exercise for your health.",
"I understand you don't want to hit the gym, but can you manage ghar ka kaam?"

Vijay comes closer to Sudha, holds her shoulders gently, and says, "We can save Maids' salary- if you want, you take that money for yourself"

Sudha's inner voice said, "the never-ending sweep-mop-cook programs.",

Sudha experienced as if she was being slapped hard and also, she broke into laughter looking at her husband's money saving program.

"She laughed—but the laugh tasted bitter."

That evening, Sudha lost herself in her thoughts, "He spends on his imported cigarettes, monthly boozing parties, purposeless reunions where it's all gossiping about colleagues, office politics, who invested where? above all, he wants me to save 3000 monthly by replacing my housemaid. what an irony?"

Probably she had a kichadi of emotions - "insult, humour, detachment".

While Vijay, on the other hand, noticed his wife becoming restless with so much free time in hand, no job. His intention was for her to keep herself busy. He knows they are soon going to have money challenges; he has a different worry. They had not shared mutually what's bothering them; instead stayed with their own assumptions and formed opinions about each other.

Sudha's Daily routine looks like,

Her day revolved around the kitchen, daughter's classes, in-laws' meals, and endless laundry. Sometimes she even skipped her own bath to reduce washing.

REFLECT

How often do we glorify housewives as 'pillars of the home' yet forget they carry invisible, unpaid shifts worth lakhs?

Just when her routine seemed endless, life whispered a new twist. That month, Sudha missed her period and she discovered she was pregnant. She was extremely happy; she had desired for second child for a long time and it had been realized now. She went through her daughter's album and recollected all the beautiful memories of her first baby's birth. She waited for the evening to share this wonderful news with her husband.

In the Evening, when Vijay returned from the office, Sudha whispered in Vijay's ears, "I am Pregnant, we are going to have a beautiful baby". Vijay managed to mask his shock, and he smiled at his wife and said, "Oh wow, but when and how this happened?".

"Where did I miss calculating her ovulation cycle, and how could I commit this blunder?" Vijay is in deep investigative thoughts.

"Vijay's panic wasn't only about the second child. Deep inside, he regretted never sitting with Sudha to plan their finances together. He realized he had carried the entire money map in his head—assuming she would just follow. He never explained, never educated, never invited her into decisions. Now, standing alone as the sole earner, every expense looked like a mountain. His concern was genuine, yet his thoughts amplified into panic and stress."

That afternoon, after many months, he took Sudha to the movie and Kerala mess, and they had a feast. Sudha was so happy and she assumed Vijay was excited to become a father for the second, time and here comes the twist.

Vijay asks, "Sudha - you know our situation- only one salary and too many expenses, responsibilities. We are happy with one kid - I want only one kid, can you abort this time?
You take your time and make your decision.

Sudha suddenly felt like puking whatever she ate for lunch, and she was taken aback, and there was extreme silence after that. She doesn't even remember when she reached home.

Sudha, in her happiness, experienced zero gravity and she was flying high. Suddenly, someone cut her wings, and she had a hard fall.

For Sudha,

"Money had become the new remote control—the person who brings the money home controls the remote"

Her thoughts were racing. "My parents managed five children, and his parents managed 4 children with one person's salary".
"Daughter's school auto driver has two kids, and his wife is housewife".
"His sister has two daughters, and his brothers had each two children",
"Then why the hell doesn't he want a second child?".
She made up her mind and declared to Vijay ..
"I am not going to drop this baby",
"I made this mistake once last year, and I will not repeat".

For Sudha, Vijay's panic looked like as if he was caught in a thousand crore rupees scam, a permanent prisoner, and he got busy with guilt trips.

He frequently repeated these dialogues to Sudha,
"Why did I ever commit this? I can never go wrong with your cycle calculation."

"Shit, it's my mistake".

Vijay is in panic; he started calculating the additional expenses of the future. Once again, both chose to stay in their thoughts and worries, not open their hearts and share their worry with each other.

Sudha is now in her 4th month; there were more scans nowadays than six years back while she was carrying her first child. Each scan, Dr visit, medicines, and buying fruits cost additional 10k.

Vijay clears his throat and says, "Sudha I think we must visit the Nursing home near our home, these corporate hospitals are charging us a bomb. He found a doctor near his home where scans can be reduced, and this thought shrank Sudha's heart.

She understands the cost getting added with her decision, but at the same time, she calculates her husband actually earns handsome amount, and she disliked his money-saving scheme only in hospital bills, not in his parties, reunion programs.

The Nursing home is decent enough, but the only change was – here, appointments are first-come First serve basis, no reservations in advance.
Dr has a minimum of 30 patients in the queue. Vijay stopped accompanying her for Dr visits as there is a long queue, he suddenly remembers taking care of his parents and daughter, and in between the juicy gossip with his friends.

Sudha is now all alone in doctor visits. Once again, she got busy in her thoughts.

"For Vijay, suggesting a smaller nursing home wasn't about neglect—it was about survival. He wished Sudha could see his fear of sinking into debt, but he didn't know how to express it without sounding miserly."

Her inner conversations, realisations were

"When I too was earning, there were Kerala mess visits, Friday movie nights, long drives, and only corporate hospitals".
"Now, as I don't earn every privilege is cut. I become Normal from Special. Even my child is treated normally. There is a change in my in-laws' behaviour towards me. They are not enquiring about me anymore, whether I had my lunch or not. Am I taking enough rest? No question asked.

The house has become like an emotionless Movie.

REFLECT

"Does money have this power to create emotions, love, care for other people?"

"When I was earning, did I experience love or attention? Am I being loved in real anytime?". Her thoughts in her brain become her own enemy- she started doubting Vijay's love for her.

She disliked this new reality.

She determined not to experience this anymore, especially her unborn child- it must be welcomed wholeheartedly. She silently started working on her resume, and within 2 weeks she received an offer letter and she immediately joined in job. She had to manage Morning sickness, sometimes feeling nausea in the middle of meetings. She has not disclosed yet in the office that she is pregnant. She wanted to do after her first month in her job.

REFLECT

"Sometimes a job offer isn't just about money—it's about dignity returning to the table."

Her job has brought joy to the family, suddenly it felt like celebrating Deepavali in January. Mother-in-law prepared Sudha's favourite payasam, and Mom-in-law took an extra effort to show off her love for bahu - by feeding a spoonful of payasam. She also started calling her in the afternoon to know if her beautiful pregnant daughter-in-law had her lunch or not. Though Sudha is happy about the shower of love but she starts observing the changing dynamics of relationships and people.

"Sudha realised affection was like a light switch—turned on or off by her payslip."

It's a life lesson for her.
She thanked the Baby and God for giving this Lesson.

Her husband Vijay, after a week of Sudha's working, brought up a conversation.
"Sudha, now you are going to enter the 6th month from now, it's very crucial for the baby, let's go to a better hospital where scans, delivery happen at one place".
For the first time in history, he did research about the best gynaecologist and the best hospital for delivery.

Sudha is again reflecting the life's lessons, changing personalities with money. She created a new equation now.

More Money Flows = More Love Flows.

This is the bitter reality. She felt like- she just drank a glass of bitter gourd juice.

Sudha was in tears and confronted Vijay - "Why is there a sudden shower of love, care and change of hospital. Is it because I'm earning money? If I am a housewife even though you could afford, why were you not ready for better hospitals?",

Vijay too was shocked at his own behaviour- he felt its logically right. more money, more comforts. He defended himself by saying - anyways, second child is only your decision, I didn't want it, yet I am supporting. You were not responsible for money when in a job - we are leading a comfortable life just because - I'm careful about money".

Pause and Reflect

Do couples plan finances together? is it only Man's job?

Have you prepared your spouse to manage finances in life without you?

Do they know about your savings, loans, insurance, and property details?

Do you live life like a permanent resident of this planet and do not bother to partner, educate spouse about finances.

Sudha is again speechless, and some truth in her husband's words hit her,

"You were not responsible with money when in job" - yes, it's true, I was.
Probably, we both could have planned finances better.

People have their perspectives; each perspective has its truth hidden in it. Do you dare to see it?

What was so true to her in her perspective was equally true for him in his perspective.
There is no one Right or Wrong; each believes their perspectives are right enough to make others feel wrong.

This creates the conflict and drama in families.

It's a conflict between Perspectives, yet it gives you the illusion of personal conflicts.

Being Emotional Vs Being Practical,

There is no one winner among Emotions and practicality - in life, both are required.

She is left with no choice than to accept her child joyfully and celebrate it with a whole heart. That was her happiest time - becoming a mother again.

Your "I love you" does not credit 100 Rs in your spouse's account automatically.
instead, love your spouse and love your skills a bit more, so that your skills credit 1000's into your account.

Myth: My money is your money in marriage.

Fact: Every person must own their finances, housewife or a working.
Love doesn't pay bills. Skills do.

CHAPTER 5

"I AM RIGHT AND YOU ARE WRONG"

Every human creation of God comes in different shapes, colours, mindsets, and attitudes—and each is unique. Yet in marriage, people often forget this uniqueness. Instead of accepting, we try to fit our spouse into the box of our definitions. Opinions and judgments take the place of acceptance, trust, and love.

These opinions become the **variables** of marriage, and each spouse builds an **equation** about the other.

The Story: Manoj & Lily

Manoj, a developer in Bangalore, and Lily, a lecturer in Mysore, were engaged and in love. Every weekend, Manoj travelled to meet her. She dressed stylishly, she welcomed him warmly, picking him up on her bike with breakfast from home. They laughed over his jokes, enjoyed movies, strolled in the park, and made each meeting memorable.

After their marriage in Bangalore, the first year was blissful—movie nights, dinners outside, weekends together with phones switched off. Manoj felt blessed: *"Lily is caring, loving, romantic—my best decision."* Lily too felt cherished: *"Manoj is transparent, funny, and always prioritises us."*

Equation in Year One:

Lily = Loving, Caring, Romantic, Laughs at every joke, Best decision of my life

Manoj = Romantic, Committed, Prioritises wife, Jovial, Transparent

But as life settled, responsibilities grew. Manoj took on home and car loans. Expenses tightened, and he worked longer hours to chase promotions and salary hikes. Sundays became his only rest day.

Lily, feeling lonely, every day she began tutoring neighbourhood children. Teaching filled her evenings with joy, but it disturbed Manoj's need for peaceful rest on sunday's. He asked her to stop tutoring; she refused. Conflicts began surfacing.

Equation in Year Three:

Lily = Loving but less attentive, Adamant, doesn't accept my requests, Short-tempered, Distant from my parents

Manoj = Workaholic, Serious, Prioritises money over marriage, less caring

The laughter of the first year had turned into complaints. Their equations had shifted.

Reflection: How Equations Change

Ask a newly married wife about her husband, and she may say:
"He is tall, handsome, friendly, never angry, always joking, and he loves me—I'm lucky."

Ask the same wife three years later, and she may reply:
"He was once friendly and loving, but now he's work-obsessed, careless about health, easily irritated, and we hardly talk."

The husband, too, shifts. What was once *"beautiful, calm, respectful, pleasing"* may become *"short-tempered, impatient, less caring."*

These equations are **dynamic**. They are not truths, but opinions shaped by time, moods, and circumstances.

Angry and tall husband

Pleasant and taller wife

Serious faced husband

Romantic wife

Kind and handsome husband

Tea lover Coffee addict

Lesson: Variables vs. Constants

Below are the **variables** based on our judgments and shifting perceptions:

Angry – Calm

Pleasant – Irritated

Serious – Silly

Romantic – Unromantic

Kind – Cruel

Tea lover – Coffee addict

Punctual and well-planned – Always late and desciplined

Follows parents' instructions – Thinks and decides independently

Careful with money and saves – Spendthrift and less savings

Frequent shopper – Hardly shops

The **constants** are the people, in their relationship: Husband + Wife in Marriages.

Yet most marriages spend years in the tug-of-war of *"I am right, you are wrong."*

The truth is—neither is right. Equations are temporary snapshots, not reality. When judgments are dropped, what remains are the constants: the two people who once chose each other.

Myth vs. Fact

- **Myth:** *"I am Right about my spouse and my spouse is wrong about me"*
  Fact: *The Equations we form about each other in Marriage are only judgments. They change with time. What remains constant is your spouse—the one you chose in your life's journey."*

Reflection for Readers

Take a pause and answer.

- What is the equation you currently hold about your spouse?
- Which parts are judgments, not truths?
- Which constants in your partner have you forgotten?
- Are you fighting to prove your equation as right—or choosing to see beyond variables?
- ✨ A strong marriage isn't built by clinging to shifting equations, but by remembering the constants: companionship, love, and the choice to walk together.

CHAPTER 6

"CONTROL YOUR SPOUSE"

Vani and Guru are just got engaged and their wedding is two months away. They stay in the same city and they see each other almost weekly. Without them actually requesting, both Vani and Guru were receiving free Knowledge transfers from their respective mothers. Accidentally mothers of both sides have the same topic going on.

Guru's mother kept on advising him -

"Do not overprotect and spend money on your future wife, she *will overpower you after marriage. You must control her well before marriage".*

On the other hand, Vani's mother advised Vani,

"Do not tell your exact salary to Guru, just tell half of it." Start doing FD of your half salary. Guru has a big family and too many expenses. He might spend your earnings too on his family.

While both sides mothers gave advice on what were their life lessons from their marriages. They want their children not to go through similar experiences those they have gone through.

"Every parent advises on marriage. But what if those words echo louder in your fights than your spouse's voice?"

Vani &Guru didn't pay any attention to what their mothers were saying, their dialogues were just registered in their brains.

Its been 11 months since Vani and Guru were married and were living in Pune. It was too far for both sets of Parents to come and stay in Pune. Vani and Guru got plenty of alone time to explore places near Pune. They were Happy.

Once Guru had a very bad day at the office, he was not in the right state and reached home from the office. Guru had a complaint about his manager, that he is being ignored and not valued enough for his work. That same day, Vani was having period cramps, and she had taken off from work. She was unable to get up from her bed and requested Guru to give her a hot water bag massage. She also mentioned, she couldn't cook anything for dinner. She also requested him to order some food.

These requests of Vani looked like demands, and Guru experienced just like his manager, even his wife doesn't respect. His mind immediately reminded his mother's relationship advice.

"How many of us still carry our parents' fears into our own marriages?"

Vani's requests felt like- she was overpowering him. He decided not to help her with any request. He just said that even he is tired and both of them slept without their dinner.

The silence, the hunger didn't allow them to sleep well; they both chose different rooms to sleep.

Vani noticed a change in Guru's behaviour. He stopped bringing groceries, fruits, which he used to do without her asking. Vani started shopping for groceries alone for her family, then onwards.

These changes of events, behaviours made Vani recollect what her mother advised her regarding salary. Vani formed an opinion that the change in Guru's behaviour is because she has not shared her full salary details and assumed that Guru needs her salary to maintain Guru's big family.

"Do we repeat our parents' marriage wounds instead of creating our own rules?"

They did not bother to clarify or question each other about their changed behaviours and days passed. Both of their disappointments, opinions piled up, and it was ready to burst open any day.

Guru always judged and validated Vani's requests. Her actions felt like she was overpowering him. His way of controlling her was to keep minimal conversations, coming late from the office, and skip home-cooked food almost every day.

REFLECT

"Have you ever mistaken your partner's pain as domination—just because someone planted that idea in your head?"

While on the other side, Vani was guessing and she was calculating in her mind when is it safe to reveal her actual salary to her husband, and she got into confusion -

"Shall I give him my fixed deposits?

"Does he want my entire salary every month?",

"D*id he marry me because I am working ?"*

REFLECT

"How many times do we assume the worst instead of asking directly?"

The unnecessary Knowledge shared by Mothers of Guru and Vani has made this couple judge and validate each others action, decisions. They stopped thriving in their relationship in just an years time.

After Constant arguments, fights over the years, on their 10th anniversary, they understood and realised how much they both were judging each other. They both reflected that the real cause of their misunderstanding was interference of their mother-in-law. Vani and Guru created a rule between themselves that they are not going to take any free advice from anyone. They both decide to work as one Team. They understood "Controlling each other in Marriage is a Myth. There must not be any ego at play between them. "

Myth:

Controlling your spouse, hiding truths, or following parental fears will protect your marriage.

Fact:

Control kills intimacy. Hiding creates suspicion. Marriage thrives only when both partners choose honesty, teamwork, and trust—free from the shadows of others' experiences.

Advice may come free, but the cost of following it blindly can be your marriage itself.

CHAPTER 7

"HAPPILY EVER AFTER"

Vijay and Rani were college sweethearts. They spent four years sneaking glances in classrooms, whispering on phone calls, and meeting at cafés, always afraid of being caught by relatives. That thrill of secrecy made their bond feel magical.

In their final year of engineering, Vijay finally gathered the courage to approach Rani's family. With trembling words, he promised them, *"I truly love her, I'll always keep Rani happy."* After some hesitation, both families agreed. Soon, with hopeful hearts, they married and moved to Bangalore for new jobs.

"What if the promise of *'I truly love her'* lasts only until life changes its script?"

The Magic Years

The early years were everything they had dreamed of. No more hiding, no more fear. They felt free—truly free—for the first time. They took "sick leave" just to spend the whole day together, laughing, talking, and discovering each other. Weekends became little escapes, and nights were filled with warmth and passion. For five years, they lived like best friends and lovers rolled into one.

On their sixth wedding anniversary, their daughter was born—a precious baby girl, the perfect gift. Rani, who had longed to be a mother, threw herself into caring for the baby. She was awake through the nights, soothing fevers, humming lullabies, forgetting her own needs. Vijay, now a rising star at work, helped when he could, but more often, he collapsed into bed, drained.

Their life looked perfect on the outside, but inside, cracks were forming.

The hugs, the long conversations, the playfulness—all began to fade.

The passion that had once been their foundation quietly slipped away.

A New Distance

When Vijay's hard work earned him a six-month assignment in the U.S., it felt like both a victory and a heartbreak. For the first time in ten years of being together, he and Rani had to live apart. Neither of them knew how much those six months would change everything.

In Texas, Vijay worked alongside two colleagues. One of them was Nisha—a bright, warm-hearted teammate, younger than him, married but stuck in a relationship that was already cracking. Her husband had moved to Australia and barely kept in touch. Nisha longed and was desperate for companionship.

At first, vijay and Nisha's bond was innocent—sharing breakfast, planning meetings, exploring new restaurants. One night, after a playful fight over the TV remote, Nisha tripped, and Vijay caught her by the waist. For a moment, their eyes locked. The laughter faded, replaced by a spark they didn't resist. Soon, they weren't just colleagues—they were lovers.

For Nisha, it felt like she had found the affection her marriage lacked. For Vijay, Nisha was vibrant, carefree, a contrast to the tired, anxious Rani back home. The line between love and betrayal blurred.

"Each night, guilt bothered him, but the thrill of escape was louder."

Rani's Shattered World

When Vijay returned to India, the affair continued in secret. He grew distant, his phone always in hand, his evenings swallowed by "work." Rani's heart ached. She remembered the man who once couldn't wait to hold her hand, who promised her forever.

Now he avoided her eyes, stopped playing with their daughter, and shut himself behind locked screens. Rani felt invisible. Every night she cried quietly, wondering:

How can love change so quickly? Is it only men who drift? Did I choose the wrong person?

She knew she had chances too—moments where she could have strayed, but she didn't.

She stayed loyal, thinking love was unshakable. The self-blame ate away at her confidence.

Desperate for answers, she hired a private investigator. Within weeks, the truth lay before her: photos, calls, secret meetings with Nisha.

When Rani confronted him, Vijay didn't deny it. "I care for both of you," he said calmly.

"You're my wife and the mother of my child, but Nisha is alone. I couldn't turn her away."

Rani's world fell apart. The man she trusted had not only betrayed her but expected her to accept it. In that moment of heartbreak, she realized something:

Love isn't about chaining someone to you, nor about tolerating what shatters your values.

One morning, after crying through all the nights, Rani woke up with a strange clarity.

She couldn't keep blaming herself for Vijay's choices.

She had given her all, and if he still strayed, it wasn't her fault.

That day, she opened her laptop and began updating her résumé. She hired a full-time maid to help with the baby and started looking for a small apartment of her own.

Rani chose not to be a victim of someone else's broken promises.

She chose to rebuild her life on her terms.

Myth:

Marriage is a "happily ever after." Once you marry and have children, love will take care of itself. Your partner belongs to you forever, no matter what.

Fact:

Love is not guaranteed. People change, life gets busier, and intimacy can fade if it isn't nurtured. Marriage is not a lifetime contract or a prison sentence—it's a daily choice to invest, connect, and stay loyal.

Love must be nourished, not assumed. And when someone stops choosing you, the bravest act of love is choosing yourself.

CHAPTER 8

THE INVISIBLE ROWDIES OF MARRIAGE — THE "SHOULDS" AND "BUTS"

The invisible rowdies of your marriage are the **"Should" and "But"** you get to hear — and use.

Confused? Want to know why I say what I say?

Let's see further...

The Ceremony of Should's

"Bride's family SHOULD have selected an AC function hall — it's too hot and sweaty like hell! You have a kanjus father-in-law."

"Groom is handsome BUT he is too short — he should have been six feet."

"Girl is darker than the groom — she SHOULD have been a little fair."

"Everything about the bride is good, BUT she is not a doctor. The groom is a doctor — he SHOULD have married another doctor."

"Sunitha, you SHOULD wear your dupatta covering your chest; no one is supposed to see the size and shape of it."

"In saree, you SHOULD bring your pallu to the front — your bum is big, you should not wear saree next time."

Sunitha got frustrated with this constant pouring of SHOULDs on her.

"What the hell? Am I the only one with a bum? You have one, your parents have — everybody's got theirs! What's the deal if it's big or small? Why should I cover with a dupatta — it's already hot! I don't want one. You go and cover your chest, your bum… whatever! Don't even tell me what I'm supposed to do."

Sunny was shocked to hear this.

He said coldly, "This is the first and last time you SHOULD never raise your voice over me or my parents."

The show had just started. 😀

The Household of Rules

"You SHOULD wake up early."

"You SHOULD prepare breakfast, pack lunch, then go to your office."
"You SHOULD NEVER call me 'Sunny' in front of my parents."
"You SHOULD NOT go shopping without me."
"You SHOULD only cook, wash dishes, sweep, mop — we NEVER had a maid before marriage. It was my mother and sister before — now it's you."
"You SHOULD NEVER talk to any male except your father or brothers — you belong to me only."
"You SHOULD stop working — my salary is enough."
"You SHOULD NOT talk to your parents every day — what's there to talk about daily?"
"You SHOULD make sure our children get all A grades."
"You SHOULD listen to me."
"You SHOULD adjust and adapt to this family — or face the consequences."
"Everything about you is good, BUT I don't like your attitude while talking to my parents."

From the time she wakes up till she sleeps, there's no shortage of SHOULDs.

Sometimes she forgets which SHOULD to follow and which to discard.

Her mind quietly asks — *"Why SHOULD I follow others' SHOULDs?"*

The Tables Turn

The flow of SHOULDs and BUTs is never one-way.

After some time, even the wife has her own share.

Sunny SHOULD receive them too. 😊

"Sunny, you SHOULD pick me up from my office in the evening."

"You SHOULD help me in the kitchen — washing dishes and drying clothes."

"You SHOULD NOT wear shorts when my friends are around."
"You SHOULD NOT talk to my friends or even look at them."
"You SHOULD tell your mother to stop reminding me of family rules every day."
"You SHOULD remember my birthday and our anniversary — never forget!"
"But you NEVER plan our trips."
"You MUST love me only and NEVER EVER cheat."
"I like everything about you, BUT you listen to your mom too much."
"I can do what you say sometimes, BUT don't ask me to listen to your mom."
"I know you love me, BUT NEVER as much as your parents."
"You earn well, BUT you don't save — you only pay your parents' loans."
"I love you, BUT you NEVER loved me enough."

The Prison We Build

The one thing that never runs out in marriage is the supply of **SHOULDs, BUTs, MUSTs, NEVERs, and EVERs.**
In fact, there's hardly a conversation without them.

The use of these words makes a person feel **compelled, imposed upon, breathless — invisible.**
It's not about the English language — each of our 1600 Indian languages has its own version of these invisible handcuffs.

Coach's Reflection: Pause and Look Within

- How many "SHOULDs" do you use with your partner each day?
- When you say *"You should,"* what are you really trying to express — love or control?
- Have your words ever made your spouse feel small, restricted, or unseen?

- Whose expectations are you carrying — yours, your parents', or society's?

The Awakening

The myth here is that one can change another person's behaviour, likes, or dislikes just by instructing them with **SHOULDs** and **MUSTs**.

It doesn't guarantee certainty in relationships — instead it shows up as forceful compliance or turns the couple as two rebels.

The fact is, when someone receives a sentence wrapped in SHOULDs and MUSTs, it creates a feeling of **force, resistance, and rebellion.**

It silently builds an **invisible prison** for both.

True love doesn't need SHOULDs to survive — it needs **awareness, respect, and trust.**

So next time you catch yourself saying "You SHOULD...,"
Pause and ask —

"Am I trying to connect, or am I trying to control?"

Myth vs Fact

Myth:

"I can make my partner change by telling them what they SHOULD or MUST do."

Fact:

"The more we impose with, the more they resist.
Love breathes freely only when control loosens its grip."

CHAPTER 9

THE WRESTLING – "YOUR PEOPLE VS MY PEOPLE"

The Story

The two foreign objects that quietly sneak into most marriages are *"Your People"* and *"My People."*
In every conflict, they wear new masks — *your parents, my parents, your sisters, my sisters, your property, my property.*
They keep changing shape but never stop dividing hearts.

Bhanu was newly married to Pradeep and had entered a joint family in Dharwad. Overnight, her world multiplied — new faces, new names, new relationships. Her memory was being tested every single day. She often found herself thinking, *"Who is this aunty again? Is she from my mother-in-law's cousin's side or father-in-law's brother's wife's side?"* It felt like a never-ending family web.

One day, a cheerful girl named Durga appeared. She smiled warmly and asked, "Tell me, who am I?"

Bhanu froze. Before she could respond, her mother-in-law jumped in enthusiastically —
"Bhanu, she is the granddaughter of my cousin brother's wife's elder brother. She couldn't attend the wedding because she had exams."

Bhanu gasped and smiled awkwardly. *What kind of puzzle was that?*
It felt as if she had been given a mental-ability question to solve — and the answer came with more confusion than clarity.

That night, she waited eagerly for her husband to return from work — the one face that felt familiar, safe, and hers.
After dinner, she sighed deeply and said, "I'm so confused and tired of remembering the names and relationships."
She had no idea what kind of conversation she was walking into.

Pradeep immediately asked, "Whose names and relationships?"

Bhanu replied innocently, "Names and relationships of the people living here."

He repeated, "Which people?"
This time, his tone was heavier — a mix of ego, hurt, and emotions that probably didn't have names in any dictionary.

Unaware of the shift, Bhanu casually said, "Ayyo, I'm talking about *your people.*"

That was all it took. The spark was lit.

Pradeep's face stiffened. "Oh, what's so difficult in remembering names? How do you remember names and relationships of *your* side then?"

And that became the **official beginning of their first conflict** — powered by two foreign bodies: *Your People* and *My People.*

From that day onward, their conversations often sounded like a courtroom debate.

From Pradeep's Side:

"What did your father give me in marriage other than 10 grams of gold and you?"
"What manners did your mother teach you — probably nothing."

"What did your parents give you as property? Now you're enjoying my parents' property."
"My mother took care of our son more than your mother."
"Your sisters are so disrespectful — just like you."
"Your brothers are fit for nothing; they don't earn enough."
"Tell your father to treat my parents well on their next visit."
"My mother cooks tastier food than you."
"Check your phone — how many times do you talk to your mother every day, and how often to mine?"

From Bhanu's Side:

"At least we gifted ten grams of gold — what did your parents give? Just five?"
"What did your mother gossip about me? And you question manners from my mother?"
"I'm not enjoying any property — come live at my parents' home then. Your property is just this old house; mine is three homes and a few extra acres."
"My mother had surgery when my son was born — she still took care of him. Who asked your mother to take care?"
"Look at your sister — she's a divorcée and stays with us. And you talk about my sisters? They're educated and settled in the USA."
"Are my brothers begging money from you? They have their lives — look at yours."
"Tell your parents not to make a scene when they visit my parents."

"Let your mother cook every day — she cooks better than I, right?"
"My mother is unwell, that's why I called her. Your mother is perfectly fine and always travelling anyway."

This list never ended.
From being newly married to twenty years into marriage, Bhanu and Pradeep continued their conversations around *your people* and *my people.*
Every argument added another layer of separation — the "we" slowly disappeared, replaced by "mine" and "yours."

Their marriage became the *longest league game*, a competition of whose side was better.
They forgot fundamentally who they were to each other — and why they shared life for twenty years, raising two children amidst these differences.

Now their children are confused too, wondering silently, *"Who are our people — Mummy's side or Daddy's side?"*
The pattern continues, inherited from the generation before them.

While fighting for *others*, both forgot who they were *to themselves.*

Reflection

As a coach, I often ask couples —

"When you fight, who are you really defending — your people or your peace?"

Your *people–my people* war is not about relatives.
It's about *ego*, *identity*, and the fear of being unseen.

Each person wants their roots acknowledged, their family respected. But when the desire to prove becomes greater than the desire to understand, connection quietly dies.

💭 **Pause and Reflect:**

- How often do you say *your parents*, *my sister*, instead of *our family*?
- When conflicts arise, are you trying to *win* or to *understand*?
- Do your children see you as one team, or two rival families under one roof?
- What would shift in your marriage if you replaced *your people* and *my people* with *our people*?

The Lesson

In trying to defend our families, we often lose the family we built together.
The moment couples start comparing who contributed more, who cooked better, whose relatives behaved well, they lose sight of *why* they came together in the first place.

Love is not a competition between two lineages.
It's a bridge that connects them.

Myth: In marriage, comparing families keeps things fair.
Fact: In the race to prove whose people are better, couples forget they are on the same side — and that's the only team that truly matters.